LOVE DROPS

An Adult Coloring Bible Study

Written by Leslie Eaton

Illustrations and Artwork by Nicole Plymesser Nelson

Bible Stories From the Heart

Bible Stories from the Heart™
Suwanee, GA

LOVE DROPS

Bible Stories from the Heart
1232 Fieldcrest Court
Suwanee, GA 30024

www.biblestoriesfromtheheart.com

Printed in the United States of America

ISBN 0998090506

Contents

Introduction

Bible Stories from the Heart incorporates reading, writing, and artwork to help you meditate and pray over God's scripture in a deep and meaningful way.

There is a reason we spend several days over the same scripture. Our Bible study is written as a way to deepen your comprehension and enhance your daily quiet time with God. It is our goal for you to savor God's word, not rush through it. We want each of you to take the time to FEEL God's love.

The study is designed to complete either with a small group or as an independent study. As an independent study, you are free to work at your own pace.

You may complete the study in a few days, a few weeks, or maybe months. ALL ARE GOOD. The important thing is to go deeper with GOD and let HIM fill your heart.

Feel free to invite a few friends to join you, or complete this study alone. Either way, get prepared for some amazing God moments through this amazing Bible study!

We would love for you to participate in our Bible Stories from the Heart group on Facebook. There, you can share your artwork, fellowship with others doing our studies and participate in our regular online studies as well. You'll be connected with a dynamic, supportive and highly engaged community of over 8,000 women. Just enter **Bible Stories from the Heart** in the Facebook search bar and you'll find us!

If you would like to purchase additional pdf files of our studies for small group use, they can be found at www.biblestoriesfromtheheart.com.

Important: if you would like to be notified of future publications and receive regular devotions, please sign up for our free email club! www.biblestoriesfromtheheart.com.

Thank you for joining us!

Meet the Writers

LESLIE EATON - Leslie will lead you through the reading and study of each lesson. She has over 20 years of experience as a professional educator. Ten of those years she served as a reading comprehension specialist. Leslie has undergone extensive training in both reading comprehension and effective learning strategies. She is now excited to bring these successful strategies to this study. Her goal is to empower people as they seek to experience God's love on a deeper level. She has led various Christian small groups and book studies in and around the Atlanta area for over 5 years. Now she is bringing her knowledge of teaching and her love of God's Word to Bible Stories from the Heart.

What to expect from Leslie:

You will be lead through each scripture lesson with one goal in mind - to know and understand God's love for you!

What we will do:

- Read Scriptures that are listed
- Reflect on the key verses contained in each lesson
- Answer discussion questions found with each lesson

What we will learn:

- Meaning of key words
- Relevant Biblical history
- Connection to our lives today

 NICOLE PLYMESSER NELSON - Nicole has been teaching art for 20 years—in elementary and high schools, retail settings, private lessons, and workshops. All along she has written her own curriculum that works for all ages and abilities. Nicole also has a successful illustration business that showcases her faith. She designs the illustrations for the studies so that all audiences will feel comfortable using art to study God's Word.

What to expect from Nicole:

The goal is for you to use art methods to meditate, pray and connect with God on an even deeper level - taking time to create will allow God to flow through your hands and fingers as you ALLOW HIS WORDS to INSPIRE YOU! As you work, pray over the images and words. Brain science shows that creating artwork actually creates more connections in the brain, making information easier to remember. You will be amazed at how this transforms your study and recall of the lessons!

Three options are available for you:

- Read the scriptures and create your own design in your Bible or journal.
- Use the coloring page versions - adding color in your media of choice.
- Or use the mini versions to trace into your Bible or faith art journal.

Why Our Studies Work

The Bible is a Book of LOVE.

If we are not careful, we may neglect to see God's Love in the scriptures that we read.

At Bible Stories from the Heart we never want this to happen. It is our goal to view every word found in the Bible as a piece of a love letter written especially for us. Because of this, we are very intentional in the way that we write and pace our lessons and art activities.

The devotions we will be studying will move us very slowly through certain passages of the Bible. In each lesson we will spend time reading and reflecting upon key words found in our focus verses. Doing this will help you to actually relate God's Word to your life and will help you to feel His love on a much deeper level.

We believe that the BEST way to study God's Word and REALLY absorb it is to take the time to reflect upon it and then allow it to flow THROUGH you as you read!!

LOVE is a verb - it is ACTION... it is not STAGNANT!!!

Consider for a minute the difference between the Dead Sea and the Sea of Galilee. Life does not exist in the Dead Sea, yet The Sea of Galilee THRIVES. What is the major difference between these two bodies of water? The Dead Sea has NO outlet and no action!

We must remember this fact and apply it whenever we spend time with the Lord.

One way to allow God's LOVE to flow through you as you study the Bible is to DOODLE or COLOR as you read.

There is something very powerful about reflecting and creating while reading.

Our Strategy: Reflective Bible Study

Each week we will focus on a different scripture. You will read and re-read that scripture several times over the week.

The purpose behind re-reading scripture is for you to intentionally spend time reflecting and meditating on God's deep and powerful love for you.

We believe that we should **meditate on the Word of God DAILY.**

We believe that the Word of God should be *savored* not gulped.

We know that the concepts in each verse are given to us from the Holy Spirit! They are meant to *guide us* and *change us.*

It is up to us to actually allow that to happen.

In order to read God's Word as intended, we must intentionally *MEDITATE* on its concepts.

David learned this in his life as did Joshua:

Psalms 119:15-16 (NKJV)
I will meditate on Your precepts and regard Your ways. I shall delight in Your statutes; I shall not forget Your word.

Joshua 1:8 (NKJV)
This Book of the Law shall not depart from your mouth, but you shall meditate in it day and night, that you may observe to do according to all that is written in it.

Our Goal

Our goal is to help you establish a deep and loving relationship with our Savior. Relationships are intentional! The best relationships develop slowly over time.

As we continue in this study, we do not want to rush through the lessons. Let's intentionally take our time and enjoy every moment that we spend in the presence of the Lord! Let's remember that <u>we are building a relationship, not earning a grade</u>. So, let's just relax and enjoy the journey!

How can we build a deeper relationship with Christ?

<u>Consider this:</u>

When you first meet a new friend or co-worker do you automatically trust this person?

Of course not! Trust is something that is built and grows over time.

The more time you spend with a person, the more time trust has to grow. As you spend time together, this new person will have various opportunities to display their loyalty, honesty, and abilities to you.

If enough of these qualities are displayed, trust begins to grow. Then every time you notice these qualities displayed again, trust grows deeper.

It is the same with God. Authentic trust is built over time. To build this trust, we must take the time to observe and discover the true character of God.

We can accomplish this by using two simple strategies:

1. Intentional Bible Study (searching for God's love)

2. Reflective Journal Writing (reflecting on God's love / S.O.A.P.)

Our Love-Directed Approach

Intentional Bible Study

Bible study which intently looks for the character traits of God is vital.

God is LOVE! God never changes! He is and will ALWAYS be LOVE!

So, what exactly is love?

1 Corinthians 13:4-8 (NKJV)
4 Love suffers long and is kind; love does not envy; love does not parade itself, is not puffed up; 5 does not behave rudely, does not seek its own, is not provoked, thinks no evil; 6 does not rejoice in iniquity, but rejoices in the truth; 7 bears all things, believes all things, hopes all things, endures all things. 8 Love never fails...

LOVE-Directed Bible Study Strategy

Read each verse of the Bible with a specific purpose - To see LOVE!

If we focus on this, we will see that EVERYTHING God has ever done or will EVER do; he does out of his intense LOVE for his children.

Wherever there is LOVE - there is God!

S.O.A.P. (Scripture, Observation, Application, Prayer)

Reflective Journal Writing

S.O.A.P. is an acronym which stands for Scripture, Observation, Application and Prayer. This technique is a powerful way to reflect on and absorb more of the verses from each lesson that speak to you.

There is a SOAP reflection page near the end of each lesson which you may use to write down your own thoughts. We've included an example below to better illustrate how the SOAP pages might be used.

The following scripture in this example is not in this study. It has been chosen for demonstration purposes.

SOAP Reflection (Scripture)

(S) Scripture:

Exodus 14:13-14 (NKJV)
13 And Moses said to the people, "Do not be afraid. Stand still, and see the salvation of the Lord, which He will accomplish for you today. For the Egyptians whom you see today, you shall see again no more forever. 14 The Lord will fight for you, and you shall hold your peace."

SOAP Reflection (Observation)

(O) Observation:

As a result of bad choices made by the Israelites, they were taken as slaves in Egypt for several years. After receiving word from God to do so, the Israelites are attempting to escape from their Egyptian captives. The Israelites are scared. They know that if they are caught they will be tortured or even killed for their rebellion.

I observe GOD'S LOVE in this verse! Moses is telling the Israelites to not be afraid, to stand firm, and that God will deliver them from their enemies. God is willing and able to lead them to safety - this is LOVE!

This verse PROVES that God was willing and able to rescue his children from hardships. Since God NEVER changes, he is still able and willing to rescue me! This strong anchor will help me stand firm when any future strong winds blow.

SOAP Reflection (Application)

(A) Application:

Just like the Israelites I made some bad choices in the past which led me into captivity. Unlike the Israelites, my captivity was more mental than physical. My mental captivity was a result of a past affair and other bad choices which surrounded that affair. As a result of these bad choices, Satan was able to temporarily bind me! During and even after the fallout from my affair, the devil worked to convince me that I was an evil person who was unworthy of love.

Even though I knew that God had forgiven me, Satan tried to keep me captive to my past. For a while I felt trapped in self - loathing! Eventually through my pain I reached out to God. I began reading and studying the Word of God like I never had before.

I had read the Bible in the past, but this time was different. This time when I read scripture I was actually reading for a purpose. My goal was to see if I was indeed unlovable! What God revealed to me was the EXACT opposite! God LOVED me more than I could ever even begin to understand. Through the blood of Christ, my past sin would not keep me shut off from his love!

This was so beautiful to me! God used water to rescue the Israelites and he used BLOOD to rescue me! I began to feel lovable again. I found that the more time I spent in God's Word the less I felt trapped in my past.

Eventually I felt totally free! God RELEASED me!

All my Lord needed was for me to grow DEEP roots in his LOVE. Then he did the rest. Now God's LOVE is able to both FILL me and FLOW through me! I now know that I am indeed LOVED!

I am now able to both receive true love and to give love.

This is because God has filled me with HIS LOVE!

I now know that nothing I will do will make my Heavenly Father love me any less!

I feel so FREE! I am no longer a CAPTIVE!

SOAP Reflection (Prayer)

(P) Prayer:

Dear Lord, thank you for loving me. Thank you for forgiving me of my past sin and setting me free! Please help me to continue to grow my spiritual roots deeper and deeper into your love. Please be with me during this study. Speak to me in bold new ways. Help me to hear and respond in positive ways to your loving voice. In Jesus name I pray, Amen.

Our God ADORES each one of us! Our God is LOVE! Take a few minutes now to write your own SOAP reflection journal entry on this same verse. As we continue in this study, let's focus our hearts and minds on GOD'S AMAZING LOVE!

We encourage you to use these "LOVE-DIRECTED" Bible study strategies throughout this study (and beyond).

Reflection Questions:

1. What am I hoping to get from this Bible Study?

2. Do I feel like I have an actual relationship with Christ? Why or why not?

3. What have I done in the past to try to build a closer relationship with God?

4. Am I willing to try a new approach to Bible Study?

Small Group Suggestions

To use this study in a small group setting we recommend the following:

1. As a group, meet one day per week.
2. Provide time for hospitality then open the group in prayer.
3. Each meeting will follow a set schedule:

Lesson Time:
- Introduce the lesson and have everyone open their workbooks. Give members about 10 minutes to read the lesson. Encourage everyone to jot down their thoughts directly on the lesson pages as they go.
- After the lesson is read, allow time for members to share their thoughts with the group.
- Then read a few discussion questions to the group and give time to discuss and provide collaborative feedback. Encourage everyone to participate.

Art Time:
- Allow time to get out all art supplies and preview the weekly art example. Members can choose to bring any art materials that they wish: watercolors, crayons, colored pencils, markers, etc. There is no one way to create the weekly art pieces.
- Members are encouraged to create their art in their own Faith Journal. Keeping the art pieces together is a wonderful way to document their spiritual growth and will make it easier for them to continue this process after this study ends.
- Play soft music in the background and allow members time to reflect on God's Word as they create their own art. You may recreate Nicole's piece exactly, or create any other picture that flows from them. If anyone is leery about their creativity, they may simply color one of the coloring sheets which are provided for each lesson.

Meeting Conclusion:
- The meeting will end with members sharing their art and thoughts with the group.
- Each member will leave the meeting with an understanding of how to use their SOAP reflection page. They will be encouraged to go deeper into God's Word in the next few days by reading the given scripture and then reflecting upon it.

As each week passes, it will become easier and more natural for members of the group to both reflect on, and interact with the Word of God.

Example Schedule

Hours of the day can be adjusted to fit your schedule.

7:00-7:30	Snacks and social time
7:35-7:40	Open in prayer and welcome members
7:40-7:50	Encourage members to interact with the text they are about to read by underlining important words and actually writing their thoughts and questions on the lesson page as they read.
7:50-8:00	Members read the weekly lesson
8:00-8:10	Read a few of the questions and allow discussion
8:10-8:15	Get out art supplies and preview weekly art piece
8:15-9:00	Play soft music and allow time for members to meditate, pray, and create their art
9:00-9:15	Share art pieces and thoughts
9:15-9:30	Pass out SOAP pages and close in prayer

Hospitality Ideas

1. Serve a light snack each week. Members can volunteer to bring finger foods or desserts on a rotating basis, if desired.

2. Offer a variety of both sugary and non-sugary drinks.

3. Have plenty of plastic cups, paper plates, as well as napkins.

4. Have name tags ready for members to fill out and wear.

5. Remember people are coming for a purpose: to connect with others and to connect with God. Be sure that all members are introduced and feel welcome.

6. Have chairs set in a circle formation to promote easy conversation throughout the lesson.

7. Provide an "ice breaker" activity for the first few meetings: there are several fun ideas found on Google (Christian small group ice breaker activities).

8. Make sure you have an area designated for the art activity. You may need to provide paper towels and plastic cups of water for watercolor paints (if needed).

9. Have a few extra boxes of crayons or colored pencils on hand in case members forget their art supplies.

Suggested Art Supplies

These are a few of Nicole's favorites but you can use any materials of your choice.

Paper: ANY kind of paper will work! Even just a basic notebook or typing paper, some may decide to do the art directly in a journaling Bible. But a separate sketchbook has several positives: you will have a book of all of your favorite verses, you can do them over and over, plus you will have space to add extra journaling as well. Canson mixed media brand is my all-time favorite due to the bright whiteness of this paper and it holds up to watercolors well.

Paints and brushes: any brand works, travel or school sets, or use the tubes of watercolor in a palette (squirt them into the pans and let them dry before use). You will want three brushes for sure: a one inch flat, a round brush, and a pointed brush.

Collage paper: Use old dictionaries from thrift stores, receipts, homework from kids, anything! Mod Podge or good old Scotch craft glue work best. Glue sticks work, but can release with watercolor on top.

Writing Utensils: There are a few different options.

- **Pen Options:** **Pilot G-2** in 10 for nice, black, even flow gel pen to journal and write prayers. **Sakura Black Glaze pens** or **Sharpie fine pen/markers** for outlining and large words.

- **Magic Rub Eraser** from Prismacolor.

- **Colored Pencils:** Prismacolor (artist grade) or Crayola (student grade) are your best bets depending on your budget.

Additional Resources

We have provided a number of additional online resources for your use.

PDF Copies of Workbooks - come in handy for those who wish to print multiple copies of the coloring pages, SOAP pages, etc. If you would like additional pdf copies of this workbook, they are available at www.biblestoriesfromtheheart.com.

Email Club - By signing up for our email club, you will receive weekly devotions, inspirational messages, art activities, exclusive offers and advance notification of new studies.

Facebook Group – if you haven't already done so, we hope you will join us on Facebook! Just type Bible Stories from the Heart into the Facebook search bar and you'll find us! You'll be connected with an engaged group of women who participate in our studies. We would love for you to post your artwork to share with the rest of the group!

Video Interview - You can learn more about our ministry by watching this video which is on the Bible Stories from the Heart YouTube page.

Bible Stories from the Heart atlantalive2016interview
Bible Stories from the Heart
2 months ago · 1,788 views
Interview on Atlanta Live explaining our faith art Bible Studies for adults

Website – where you will find more information on our Facebook group, art tutorials, coloring pages and more: **www.biblestoriesfromtheheart.com**

Art Examples

You also must BE READY because the SON of MAN will COME at an hour when you do not expect HIM.

Luke 12:40

Nicole Plymesser Nelson 2016

the LORD is MY STRENGTH & MY SONG HE HAS GIVEN ME VICTORY.

EXODUS 15:2

www.nicplynel.com

In Him our hearts Rejoice for we trust in His Holy name.

Psalm 33:21

Nicole Plymesser Nelson 2016

This is my comfort in my distress – that your promise gives me life.

Psalm 119:54

Nicole Plymesser Nelson 2016

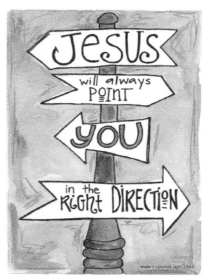

JESUS will always POINT YOU in the RIGHT DIRECTION

www.nicolynel.com 2016

Devotion One

Focus Verses

Luke 12:35-40 (NKJV)

<u>The Faithful Servant and the Evil Servant</u>

35 "Let your waist be girded and your lamps burning; 36 and you yourselves be like men who wait for their master, when he will return from the wedding, that when he comes and knocks they may open to him immediately. 37 Blessed are those servants whom the master, when he comes, will find watching. Assuredly, I say to you that he will gird himself and have them sit down to eat, and will come and serve them.38 And if he should come in the second watch, or come in the third watch, and find them so, blessed are those servants. 39 But know this, that if the master of the house had known what hour the thief would come, he would have watched and not allowed his house to be broken into. **40 Therefore you also be ready, for the Son of Man is coming at an hour you do not expect."**

History

In Biblical times, men and women typically wore long robes throughout the day. This made the duties of servants rather difficult to complete at times. To help with this, servants would often keep their robes tucked into the belts around their waist. This is where the phrase, "let your waist be girded" originated. This phrase was common in those days. It is referring to how servants should remain dressed and ready to serve their masters at all times.

Even if the master was away for a while, the servants were to remain totally FOCUSED on their master. They were to always remember that they were indeed the servant. Even while the master was away they continued to be the servant, their role did not change! They were never to consider themselves to be an off duty servant or worse yet a stand-in master. It was their continuous job to take care of their TRUE master's business while he traveled and to stay girded and ready for when he returned!

Connection to Us

As Christians, we are to consider ourselves to be God's servants. We are to have a servant's heart; not only toward our fellow man but also toward our Lord.

Our focus verses for today are referring to this. Our verses are reminding us of the importance of maintaining a servant's heart and mind-set toward our Lord and Savior (our MASTER) at all times. We must be always ready to both RECEIVE God's love and direction - and then GIVE God's love wherever and however he directs us.

Like the servant in our focus verses, we too need to be "girded and ready" at all times to serve our master. But how can we do this?

As we reflect upon our verses, we will find that the phrase, "girded and ready" is referring more symbolically towards our hearts and minds rather than literally towards our clothing and appearance.

Just as servants in Biblical times needed to keep their robes in "ready position," we to need to also keep our hearts and minds in "ready position."

To do this we must be ever aware of the needs around us and stay tuned-in to Christ each and every day!

One way to help us do this is for us to frequently ask our Savior how we can SERVE Him. To be girded and ready means to be ALWAYS open and listening for our master's voice. It means to continuously remember our intended position - we are the servant and God is our master! We are to FIRST focus our hearts on HIM and HIS plans. THEN we should strive to keep HIS HOUSE in order. Our goal is to stand PREPARED and READY - excited and anticipating our master's return!

Focus Words

At Bible Stories from the Heart we believe that EVERY word in the Bible was dictated by GOD himself. Because of this we intentionally spend time each week studying key words from our focus verse. Our goal is to go DEEPER into God's Word. We want to FEEL HIS LOVE for us in each and every beautiful word of scripture!

We strive to do this through word study reflection activities.

As you continue in this lesson you will see a reflection activity for you to complete. With this activity, we encourage you to read the entire weekly focus verses again. As you re-read the verses, concentrate as deeply as you can on the key words for this activity.

Seek to make personal connections and write them down. Pray to your Heavenly Father to reveal new truths to you. You will be amazed what God will show you through this easy activity. Repeat this activity several times over this coming week.

Reflection Activity

Luke 12:40
Therefore, you also be ready, for the Son of Man is coming at an hour you do not expect.

Be- γίνομαι- ginomai: to cause to be.
Be- (verb) cause to occur

Ready- ἔτοιμος- hetoimos: ready, prepared
Ready- (adjective) in a suitable state for an activity, action, or situation; fully prepare

Connection Activity

The words "be ready" are very important. They go together to describe how we should strive to exist on a daily basis. We do not need to overlook these vital words. Remember, they were specifically given to us by our Lord and master: Our Heavenly Father.

In this verse God is giving us direct instructions on how to live. Consider this fact: to "be ready" requires action on our part. Reflect and pray over those words for a few minutes.

Ask God to speak to specific areas of your life that may need help becoming ready.

What is God revealing to you?

What are some actions that you can take today to prepare for your master's return? Are there some areas of your master's house (your heart) that need cleaning? Do you need to restock some needed supplies and housewares to get your master's house (your heart) in tip top shape? Do you need a fresh supply of love, forgiveness, patience? Are there possessions that you need to stop obsessing over or fretting about? In other words, do you need to "declutter" your mind from love of "things" to open up more space for love of God?

Take the next few minutes to draw an outline of a house (to represent your heart) inside your house write down any specific areas of readiness that God reveals to you. For example, if God reveals that you need to be girded by being more open to Him - draw a welcome mat inside your door and write a message asking God to help you OPEN your heart.

If you feel that you need to spend more time reading God's Word - draw an image inside your house which represents that. Ask God to help you free your mind of any distractions or worldly pulls that would lead you away from daily Bible reading. You may want to even draw a trashcan and place drawings of any distractions that God reveals to you inside the trashcan.

If you need to spend more time in prayer - draw a picture to represent that. Sketch a representation of you "praying." Add this sketch many places inside your house. Beside EVERY sketch of you praying, draw a picture to represent God's presence- this can be a cross, a heart, a throne, God's mighty hand reaching out to you, etc. This will be a good reminder that God is RIGHT beside you at all times. HE IS ALWAYS ENGAGED and ALWAYS LISTENING! Keep this visual with you throughout this week and all throughout this study.

Any time God reveals a new area of readiness to you - add it to your picture and PRAY over it. We want to intentionally do our part to be girded and READY when our master returns! He is willing and ready to help us - all we need to do is ASK and obey.

Ready or Not
By Deborah Ann Belka

When the Lord comes,
where will you be
what will you be doing
will the clouds you see?

Will you be able to hear,
the last trumpet call
or will it on deaf ears
plummet and fall?

When the Lord comes,
what will you be thinking
will you be prepared . . .
or miss the twinkling?

Will you be alert,
at any given instant
or will you be asleep
far off and distant?

When the Lord comes,
will you be ready or not
will you be waiting . . .
in the clouds to be caught?

~~~~~~~~~~~

Copyright 2015
Deborah Ann Belka

https://poetrybydeborahann.wordpress.com

Devotion One Discussion Questions

1. What is your big takeaway from this week's lesson?

2. Do you think most people prepare more for out of town company coming to their house than their LORD and SAVIOR coming back? Why?

3. Do you think it is sometimes easy to forget that we are the SERVANTS and that God is our MASTER? Why?

4. Do you consider the word servant to be a positive or negative word in relation to us and Christ? Why?

5. What do you think most people fail to do on a daily basis in order to "BE GIRDED"?

6. What are you going to strive to do from this point forward as a result of studying this scripture?

Devotion One SOAP Activity

For your weekly SOAP activity, you are encouraged to choose ANY verse from the weekly focus verses to reflect deeper upon. Here are our weekly verses again:

Luke 12:35-40 (NKJV)

The Faithful Servant and the Evil Servant

35 Let your waist be girded and your lamps burning; 36 and you yourselves be like men who wait for their master, when he will return from the wedding, that when he comes and knocks they may open to him immediately. 37 Blessed are those servants whom the master, when he comes, will find watching. Assuredly, I say to you that he will gird himself and have them sit down to eat, and will come and serve them. 38 And if he should come in the second watch, or come in the third watch, and find them so, blessed are those servants. 39 But know this, that if the master of the house had known what hour the thief would come, he would have watched and not allowed his house to be broken into. 40 Therefore you also be ready, for the Son of Man is coming at an hour you do not expect.

To help get you started, here is an example SOAP that I did based on this week's scripture. I chose verse 39. There is a SOAP page for you to use in doing your own reflective writing after this example.

(S) Scripture

Luke 12:39 *But know this, that if the master of the house had known what hour the thief would come, he would have watched and not allowed his house to be broken into.*

(O) Observation

I noticed that this section of scripture is titled, "The Faithful Servant and the Evil Servant." As I read and reflect upon verse 39 I understand why this title applies. Verse 39 helps me to see that Jesus is describing the attitudes of two different people through this story. In this parable, the faithful servant is considered faithful because this servant knows his place and knows his master. Whereas the evil servant is considered evil because he thinks himself to be the "master" of his house. He does not truly know HIS TRUE MASTER at all.

This evil servant considers Jesus to be a THIEF! When Jesus returns, this servant feels violated and intruded upon instead of excited and fulfilled.

(A) Application

The world in which we live encourages us to OBTAIN more and more possessions. Our society tries to trick us into believing that we can and should OWN lots of amazing THINGS while here on earth. This earthly thinking is what caused the evil servant in our focus verse to become confused. NOTHING we have belongs to us! We are NOT masters - we are SERVANTS! Verse 39 reminds us of this. None of these earthy items

actually belong to us! Out of ALL of our so-called possessions, 100% of them belong to God. We must understand and believe this to be true! God is the owner and MASTER of everything. God, our MASTER, has simply entrusted us, HIS SERVANTS, to watch over HIS things until he returns. We are NOT masters of our possessions! I need to remind myself of this daily!

(P) Prayer

Dear Heavenly Father please guide my thoughts and desires. Help me to gird myself daily to stand ready to do your will! Please forgive me for oftentimes thinking that I am the master of my life and possessions instead of you. Please help create in me more of a servant's heart. Thank you for loving me☺
Now it is your turn to SOAP!

Bible Stories
From the Heart

Scripture:_____
_____
_____
_____
_____
_____

Observation:_____
_____
_____
_____
_____
_____

Application:_____
_____
_____
_____
_____
_____

Prayer:_____
_____
_____
_____
_____
_____

You also must BE READY because the SON of MAN will COME at an hour when you do not expect HIM.

Luke 12:40

Nicole Plymesser Nelson 2016

Devotion Two

Focus Verses

Exodus 15: 1-2 (NKJV)

The Song of Moses

1 Then Moses and the children of Israel sang this song to the Lord, and spoke, saying: "I will sing to the Lord, For He has triumphed gloriously! The horse and its rider He has thrown into the sea! **2 The Lord is my strength and song, And He has become my salvation; He is my God, and I will praise Him; My father's God, and I will exalt Him.**

History

Notice that the title of our focus verses for this week is "The Song of Moses."

It is interesting to note that The Song of Moses is the first song recorded in the Bible. This song was written and sung by Moses after God had set him and the Israelites FREE. This song was a very passionate and powerful song of deep celebration.

Why were the Israelites celebrating? They had been held as slaves in Egypt for over 400 years and now they were FREE! God had destroyed their captors and provided them with a fresh, new start!

God not only set the Israelites free, but he did so in a huge and monumental way. Our mighty and powerful God actually parted the Red Sea to help his children escape from their captors! As the dry land appeared, Moses was able to lead the Israelites right down the middle of the Red Sea! This is amazing!

Then just as the song describes when the Israelites were safely on the other side, God released the waters of the sea. As the powerful waters of the Red Sea remerged, the evil Egyptians drowned. The Israelites were now FREE! This true story is indeed truly "song worthy."

Connection to Us

Just as God did not want captivity for the Israelites, he does not want captivity for any of his children today. God LOVES us! He wants us to live in freedom and peace under HIS incredible LOVE - not under the captivity and destruction of sin.

To help us resist sin's captivity let's learn from the Israelites. Earlier in the Bible the Israelites made some bad choices. Because of those bad choices they found themselves taken as captives in Egypt. We must realize that if we are not careful, the same thing can happen to us today. If we are not careful, we too will find ourselves bound in captivity! Our bad choices may not lead us captives in Egypt, but we will easily find ourselves captive to our sin!

The good news is - God LOVES US! If we turn to him and sincerely ask for help, God can rescue us from captivity as well! God can free us from our sin and place us once again under his freedom and showers of Heavenly LOVE!

If we allow God to lead us out of our captivity, we too will be FREED and ready to receive God's LOVE! Just like the celebration of our focus verses for today, our freedom should also be seen as a CELEBRATION! Do you think we sometimes take our "Red Sea" rescues from sin for granted? If so, maybe it is time for some of us to CELEBRATE! Maybe it is time for some of us to reflect on some of our own God given freedom rescues and actually SING- just like Moses!

Notice when God rescued the Israelites destruction happened in the process. This huge detail does not need to be overlooked. The pathway back to the Israelites bondage was destroyed when God freed them! Upon gaining freedom, The Israelites did not then try to swim back to the land of their captivity (Egypt). They rejoiced in their freedom and walked FORWARD in their fresh start!

We need to let this really sink in. When God rescues us from bondage he is wanting us to consider the pathway back to that sin destroyed! We are not to look back! We are not to return to our captivity! We are to rejoice in our freedom and move FORWARD - just as the Israelites did!

Focus Words

At Bible Stories from the Heart we believe that EVERY word in the Bible was dictated by GOD himself. Because of this, we intentionally spend time each week studying key words from our focus verse. Our goal is to go DEEPER into God's Word. We want to FEEL HIS LOVE for us in each and every beautiful word of scripture! We strive to do this through word study reflection activities.

As you continue in this lesson you will see a reflection activity for you to complete. With this activity, we encourage you to read the entire weekly focus verses again. As you reread the verses, concentrate as deeply as you can on the key words for this activity. Seek to make personal connections and write them down. Pray to your Heavenly Father to reveal new truths to you. You will be amazed what God will show you through this easy activity. Repeat this activity several times over this coming week.

Reflection Activity

Exodus 15:2 (NKJV)

<u>The Song of Moses</u>

The Lord is my strength and song, And He has become my salvation; He is my God, and I will praise Him; My father's God, and I will exalt Him.

Strength - עוז עז: oze, force, security, majesty, praise

Song - זמרת: zimrâth, instrumental music; by implication praise

Salvation - ישועה: yesh-oo'-aw, deliverance; hence aid, victory, prosperity

God - אל: ềl, shortened from strength; as mighty; especially the Almighty

Exalt - רום: rûm to raise, lift, lift up, take up, set up, erect, exalt, set on high

Connection Activity

Think about the word "exalt". This word is a verb. It requires action on our part. But, what does it truly mean to exalt someone? How can we intentionally exalt God?

To exalt someone means to lift them up with words, or to speak highly of, so to exalt God we must speak highly of him! To do this, we must SHARE all of our amazing revelations and experiences God with others anytime we feel led to do so!

God may not part seas around us on a daily basis, but he is ALWAYS with us!

His hand is ALWAYS near. He is always showering us with HIS LOVE, but sadly, we are oftentimes too busy or distracted to notice HIM. This is a tragedy! How can we celebrate and EXALT him if we do not notice HIS PRESENCE in our daily life?

Starting today let's take some specific action steps to fix this!

The first step to exalting God is to first intentionally LOOK for HIM every moment of every day. When we see his hand moving in our life no matter how big or small, let's document it!

Action Step

One way to document God's hand in our lives is to keep a "Divine Diary". Just as young girls keep diaries to help them remember and celebrate special moments, we can do the same as adults! Instead of our childhood diaries where we would write about all of the boys that we had crushes on, let's instead write about GOD! Our adult diary will be more of a "God Moment" Diary.

This "Divine Diary" can be either a calendar or journal. This special diary will be an intentional way for us to NOTICE and then forever remember all of the special moments between us and God!

If you want to take it one step farther, you can even create a "HEAVENLY MEMORY BOX." In this box you can keep anything that reminds you of a special God moment. For example, a key from a house God blessed you with (maybe write the date you obtained the house on the key), a receipt of a bill God helped you pay off, a medical bracelet from your last hospital stay because God HEALED you, the pregnancy test which showed that God had blessed you with your first child, etc.

As a way to exalt God, let's be ready at a moment's notice to "share" one or more of these special God Moments and amazing memories with the people around us.

It is SO INCREDIBLE that The God of the Universe chooses to touch our lives on a daily basis! We need to do all we can to NOTICE and EXALT him for this!

Are you ready to see God's LOVE for you in a bold new way?

If so, I challenge you to begin keeping your "Divine Diary" TODAY!

The page which follows will help you start your "Divine Diary."

We recommend keeping a "Divine Diary" on a calendar of some sort.

Divine Diary

Use a notebook or journal to document all of your
Special GOD MOMENTS

If you hear a word from God, write it down.
Write down the exact DAY/DATE/TIME you hear it.

If a prayer gets answered, write it down.
Write down the DAY/DATE/TIME it happens.

If you FEEL God's love in a new and special way,
Write down EXACTLY what you feel, sense and see.
Document the moment as much as possible
along with the DAY/DATE/TIME.

GOD MOMENTS Are SPECIAL!
Each one should be
NOTICED, DOCUMENTED and CELEBRATED!

Bible Stories
From the Heart

God of Our Strength
By Deborah Ann Belka

God of our strength,
God of our hope
give us each day
the power to cope.

Give us the wisdom,
give us perseverance
help us to keep running
with faith and assurance.

God of our salvation,
God of our redemption
give us the boldness
when facing rejection.

Give us the courage,
give us the fortitude
help us to reflect You
in our daily attitude.

God of our strength,
God of our enlightenment
we need Your power. . .
in today's environment!

~~~~~~~~~~

Devotion Two Discussion Questions

1. What is your big "takeaway" from this week's lesson?

2. Why do you think it is important for our spiritual growth to EXALT God?

3. How does today's scripture demonstrate God's LOVE for his children?

4. Do you have a sin in which you feel captive? If so, what do you desire God to do to help free you?

5. God closed the waters back so that the Israelites would see that the path back to their captivity was gone. What doors of sin and captivity has God tried to close for you?

Devotion Two SOAP Activity

For your weekly SOAP activity, you are encouraged to choose a focus verse from this week or a related verse to reflect deeper upon.

Here are a few choices:

Our focus verse

Exodus 15:2 (NKJV)

The Song of Moses

The Lord is my strength and song, And He has become my salvation; He is my God, and I will praise Him; My father's God, and I will exalt Him.

Related verses

Isaiah 12:2 (NKJV)
Behold, God is my salvation; I will trust, and not be afraid: for the LORD JEHOVAH is my strength and my song; he also is become my salvation.

Isaiah 25:1 (NKJV)
O LORD, thou art my God; I will exalt thee, I will praise thy name; for thou hast done wonderful things; thy counsels of old are faithfulness and truth.

2 Samuel 22:47 (NKJV)
The LORD liveth; and blessed be my rock; and exalted be the God of the rock of my salvation.

Bible Stories
From the Heart

Scripture:_____

_____
_____
_____
_____
_____

Observation:_____

_____
_____
_____
_____
_____

Application:_____

_____
_____
_____
_____
_____

Prayer: _____

_____
_____
_____
_____
_____

Devotion Three

Focus Verses

Psalm 119: 49-50 (NKJV)
49 Remember the word to Your servant, upon which You have caused me to hope.
*50 **This is my comfort in my affliction, For Your word has given me life**.*

History

Our focus verse for this week comes from Psalm 119 which is the longest chapter written in our Bible and the longest song recorded in God's Word. It contains an astounding 176 verses. Most of these verses focus on actually praising God's Word. This is important: Remember that God himself chose every word that would be written in HIS Holy Word, and HE chose that the longest chapter would be about the importance of HIS WORD! Not only its importance, but also its hope and comfort! It is through his Word that we have a LOVE-FILLED life!

It is through his Word that we are shown both how to feel and understand true LOVE! It is through his Word that we learn how to not only receive God's love but also how to share God's love with others!

This psalm was written to remind us of the importance of reading and reflecting on God's Word. Remember: God's Word represents God's LOVE! We are not told who authored this psalm, but some people believe that each verse was authored by a different person. These same people think that this psalm was written during the Israelites time of captivity in Babylon. If this is the case, that means that each verse speaks of a different individual's feelings about God's Word and what is means to THEM - this is BEAUTIFUL!

If we were to write a statement in our journal explaining the importance of God's Word to US personally, what would WE write? Can we connect personally with any of the verses written in this psalm?

Connection to Us

How many of us consider the reading of God's Word to be a chore? Through Psalm 119, God is trying to change our view. Through these many verses God is challenging each one of us to change our perspective. Through these stanzas, He is teaching us to consider Bible study a blessing.

How many of us if we are thirsty view water as a blessing, or if we are hungry view bread as a gift? Let's pray to our Heavenly Father to help as view daily Bible reading with this same desire and fulfillment. Daily Bible reading can actually FILL us with LOVE: both with God's LOVE and LOVE for others! Let's ask God to shower us with His incredible "Love Drops" (words of LOVE) each and every time we read His Word.

Focus Words

As you continue in this lesson you will see a reflection activity for you to complete. With this activity, we encourage you to read the entire weekly focus verses again. As you reread the verses, concentrate as deeply as you can on the key words for this activity.

Seek to make personal connections and write them down. Pray to your Heavenly Father to reveal new truths to you. You will be amazed what God will show you through this easy activity. Repeat this activity several times over this coming week.

Reflection Activity

Psalm 119: 49-50 (NKJV)
49 Remember the word to Your servant, upon which You have caused me to hope. 50 This is my comfort in my affliction, For Your word has given me life.

Affliction - עני: *on-ee'* -depression, that is, misery

Your word - אמרה אמרה: *im-raw', em-raw'*- **commandment**, speech, word.
It is important to note that **commandments** in the Bible are simply Godly directions for how to live in accordance with God's will. God's **commandments** should not be viewed as negative or restrictive, because they are quite the opposite. God's **commandments**, "Mitzvah" are given to us by God to help us live lives that have the least amount of pain and distress as possible. God's Mitzvah center around LOVE. They help guide us in establishing and keeping healthy emotional lifestyles and relationships. God LOVES us. Through his "Mitzvah" he is showing us how to live peaceful and love - filled lives. God's **commandments** are perfect examples of incredible and Heavenly "Love Drops"!

Life - חיה: *châyâh* -to *live*, whether literally or figuratively; to *revive*

Connection Activity One

Read our focus verse again replacing some of the key words with synonyms:
This is my relief in my depression, For Your Heavenly "Love Drops" of guidance have revived me.

Many times depression and affliction are caused by relationship problems. Think about a time when you have felt the sadness of a broken relationship. God created us to be relational beings. He guides us through his Word to know how to develop healthy relationships. It is up to us to read and apply this guidance. To help with this we may need to change our opinion of the word commandments. Spend the next few minutes reflecting on this word.

Ask God to help change any negative thinking that you may have towards this word. Pray to your Heavenly Father to continue to call to you to read his Word and understand both the LIFE and LOVE that are behind his commandments. Thank him for always wanting what is best for you.

Ask him to help his Holy "Love Drops "(Commandments) to be permanently imprinted in your brain. Ask him to continuously lead you toward true happiness which can only be found through loving and healthy relationships.

Connection Activity Two

How has doing this study and spending time in God's Word revived you thus far? Take a few minutes to reflect upon this question. If you had any special moments that you can attribute to God this week, take a few minutes to write them down in your "Divine Diary" adding as much detail as possible.

Take a few minutes to connect your special God moments to our verse for this week. How has spending time in scripture comforted you this week? Were you able to make a good relationship-based decision this week by looking to God's commandments for guidance? If so, how would the outcome have been different if you had not turned to God for guidance? Take a few minutes now to thank God for his loving commandments and for always wanting what is best for you.

If you are having a relationship issue in your life, now is the time to pray for God's help and guidance in this situation. If you are feeling a heavy relationship type of burden today, I challenge you to try completing a "prayer drawing" activity at this time to help you.

Sometimes by drawing and doodling as we pray, we will actually be doing our part to quiet our hearts and minds enough to be able to focus on God's love more intently. You may find that the physical act of moving your hand as you pray may actually allow God's LOVE and thoughts to FLOW through you more freely.

I challenge you to try this "prayer doodling" activity on the following page and see if it helps you in any way:

Prayer Doodling

1. As you pray, ask God to open your heart to him in a bold new way. As you pray these words, draw a big heart in the middle of your page.

2. Next, ask God to forgive you for any relationship breaking sins that you could have committed recently - both ones you are aware of and ones that you may have chosen to not "remember."

3. Then, write those sins OUTSIDE of the heart that you drew. Also, write the NAMES of people that you may have offended OUTSIDE of the heart.

4. Pray and ask for forgiveness for EACH individual sin.

5. Each time you pray, cross off that sin and MOVE the person's name INSIDE the heart.

6. At the conclusion of your prayer, ask God to guide you in what you need to do next.

7. If God leads you to call or go visit one or ALL of the people that you offended to apologize - DO IT! Now is the time to CLEAN out your heart!

8. Thank God for loving you. Thank him for forgiving you. Ask him to help you develop and grow stronger and more loving relationships. Ask him to fill you COMPLETELY with HIS LOVE! COMFORT, LOVE, and LIFE are ALL interrelated - ask God to always help you to ALWAYS remember this!

My Comfort Rests

By Deborah Ann Belka

Holy Spirit, my comfort rests,
upon the bosom of Thy breast
You soothe me when I'm in need
I am calm, when to You I heed.

I call out to Thee, upon my bed,
thoughts of peace fill my head
into Thy hands my soul now rests
in Your stillness, I feel blessed.

Oh, my Comforter my fears relieve,
so Thy tranquility, I may receive
come yet closer to me as I pray
show me the truth, light and way.

Holy Spirit, my comfort rests,
You'll not hear, my protests . . .
abide with me forever more
be my anchor, my soul's moor!

~~~~~~~~~~~~

John 14:16

Devotion Three Discussion Questions

1. What are some issues that have caused you to feel depression or affliction lately?

2. People normally feel the least amount of depression when they have strong and healthy relationships with other people. Why do you think this is?

3. How do you think God's commandments give us comfort?

4. Do you think we sometimes ask for comfort even though we are causing affliction in our lives? Should we expect to feel comfort when we choose to go against God's Words (commandments)? What do you think God would say to us about this?

5. What do you think God is wanting to reveal to you through this week's devotion?

Devotion Three Soap Activity

For your weekly SOAP activity, you are encouraged to choose our focus verse from this week or a related verse to reflect deeper upon.

Here are a few choices:

Our focus verse

Psalm 119: 49-50 (NKJV)
*49 Remember the word to Your servant, upon which You have caused me to hope. 50 This is my comfort in my **affliction**, For **Your word** has given me life.*

Other related verses

2 Corinthians 1:4 (NKJV)
Who comforts us in all our tribulation, that we may be able to comfort those who are in any trouble, with the comfort with which we ourselves are comforted by God.

Psalm 23:4 (NKJV)
Yea, though I walk through the valley of the shadow of death, I will fear no evil; For You are with me; Your rod and Your staff, they comfort me.

Bible Stories
From the Heart

Scripture:_____
_____
_____
_____
_____
_____

Observation:_____
_____
_____
_____
_____
_____

Application:_____
_____
_____
_____
_____
_____

Prayer:_____
_____
_____
_____
_____
_____

This is my
Comfort
in my
distress—
that your
promise
gives
me
life.
Psalm 119:50

Nicole Plymesser Nelson 2016

Devotion Four

Focus Verses

John 12:26 (NKJV)
26 If anyone serves Me, let him follow Me; and where I am, there My servant will be also. If anyone serves Me, him My Father will honor.

History

When Jesus was alive on earth he lived as a servant. The Lord God in heaven was Jesus' master. Jesus served God by following GOD'S will each and every moment. Jesus lived to SERVE!

We must do the same! But who should we serve? Not ourselves, or anyone other than God, this will only lead us to misery and emptiness. We must only serve God by continuously following Jesus.

This is God's ultimate plan for order and happiness. Our world is designed to have God as the ONE AND ONLY MASTER of all. Jesus understood this. It is important for us to understand this as well.

God, as master, is a common theme in the Bible. In several Biblical scriptures, God is actually called Adonai (a-do-NI). Adonai comes from the word, adon, which is a Hebrew word meaning lord. This word refers to a human who is a superior, master or owner. Adonai is the plural form of adon and always refers to God as Lord, Master and Owner. But, the name Adonai also implies a relationship: God is our Lord and Master only if we are his servants. We must choose to serve him! Jesus lived on earth to serve God, we must follow Jesus and do the same.

Connection to Us

In our culture to serve or obey a person often means putting ourselves in a demeaning or humiliating position. In our society, the thought of "serving" another person invokes very negative images. This should not be the case when we think of "serving" God. It is vital for us to change our view of these words. For our own well-being and ultimate happiness, we must understand that BOTH of these words "service" and "obedience" are in fact POSITIVE words - WHEN REFERRING TO GOD!

Serving God is totally different than being a servant of another human being. It is only when we serve God that we are truly fulfilled, and it is when we obey him that we are truly blessed. This is a powerful truth that is ultimately hard for our human minds to understand.

How can living as a servant be fulfilling? To help us understand let's first consider just who our Lord God actually is - God is LOVE! This is a huge fact that we do not need to overlook.

When we are serving God and following Jesus, we are in fact serving and following LOVE! By "serving" LOVE, we are in essence feeding LOVE and helping the kingdom of LOVE grow! It is when we are "serving" love here on earth that we ultimately feel fulfilled - it is what we were created to do. Jesus understood this. We must intentionally follow his lead.

Focus Words

As you continue in this lesson you will see a reflection activity for you to complete. With this activity, we encourage you to read the entire weekly focus verses again. As you reread the verses, concentrate as deeply as you can on the key words for this activity.

Seek to make personal connections and write them down. Pray to your Heavenly Father to reveal new truths to you. You will be amazed what God will show you through this easy activity. Repeat this activity several times over this coming week.

Reflection Activity

John 12:26 (NKJV)
26 If anyone serves Me, let him follow Me; and where I am, there My servant will be also. If anyone serves Me, him My Father will honor.

Serves - διακονέω: diakoneō to minister, serve, do service

Follow - ἀκολουθέω: akoloutheō properly, to be in the same way with, i.e. to accompany (specially, as a disciple)

There - ἐκεῖ: ekei there, in that exact place

Honor - τιμάω: timaō to prize, that is, fix a valuation upon; by implication to revere

Notice that this verse states that God will honor us if we serve him - this is HUGE! To honor means to show and feel esteem, value, or great respect toward another person.

So, in essence when we replace some key words in this verse with related synonyms, this verse is saying - **if we minster/serve (SHOW LOVE) in the same way as Jesus did; that God the Father will feel great esteem, value, and respect toward us! This is AMAZING!**

By serving God we will be helping LOVE grow and we will be earning the respect of GOD himself! This fact in itself should make us feel fulfilled and happy at any given moment.

Connection Activity

Trace a picture of your hand. On the palm write all of the ways that you can serve God (spread LOVE) this upcoming week.

For example, if you can cook - write that. If you can share encouraging words - write that. If you can lend a hand to someone who is weak or hurt - write that, etc.

Pray to God to reveal some names to you that will be in need of HIS LOVE this week.

On each finger (or as many as you can) write the name of the person that God reveals to you.

Carry this picture in your purse or pocket throughout the week. ADD names to your hand throughout the week anytime God reveals a new "need" to you.

Some people are needing GOD'S LOVE and God is wanting to use YOUR HAND to disperse that LOVE this week.

Are you ready to be open and available to God?

You will find that the MORE love you give away, the MORE love you will be FILLED with! It is AMAZING, but TRUE! We actually were CREATED TO LOVE! God designed each of us in our own UNIQUE and AMAZING LOVE-DISPERSING way!

Matthew 22:36-39 (NKJV)
36 "Teacher, which is the great commandment in the law?" 37 Jesus said to him, "'You shall love the LORD your God with all your heart, with all your soul, and with all your mind. 38 This is the first great commandment. 39 And the second is like it: 'You shall love your neighbor as yourself."

I Put God Before Me
By Deborah Ann Belka

I put my God before me,
I let Him lead my way
I know I can trust Him
to guide me every day.

I hold tight to His right hand,
He grabs onto my left one
He slowly pulls me upwards
till I get closer to His Son.

My soul finds refreshment,
in hope I find true rest
His peace lets me know
just how much I'm blessed.

My way is paved in mercy,
joy follows me where I go
His presence in my life
I shall forever know!

~~~~~~~~

Copyright 2013
Deborah Ann Belka

https://poetrybydeborahann.wordpress.com

Devotion Four Discussion Questions

1. What is your big takeaway from this week's lesson?

2. What connection can you make between this week's scripture and the title of this series "Love Drops"?

3. Why do you think we have such a negative image of the word "servant"?

4. How is God different from any other "lord" or "master" that you have ever heard of?

5. How does serving God actually fulfill us?

6. What are your gifts? Do you feel more fulfilled when you use your gifts to spread God's love? If so, give an example.

Devotion Four SOAP Activity

For your weekly SOAP activity, you are encouraged to choose our focus verse from this week or a related verse to reflect deeper upon. Here are a few choices:

Our focus verse

John 12:26 (NKJV)
If anyone serves Me, let him follow Me; and where I am, there My servant will be also. If anyone serves Me, him My Father will honor.

Related verses

Romans 12:1-2 (NKJV)

Living Sacrifices to God

1 I beseech you therefore, brethren, by the mercies of God, that you present your bodies a living sacrifice, holy, acceptable to God, which is your reasonable service. 2 And do not be conformed to this world, but be transformed by the renewing of your mind, that you may prove what is that good and acceptable and perfect will of God.

Hebrews 6:10 (NKJV)
For God is not unjust to forget your work and labor of love which you have shown toward His name, in that you have ministered to the saints, and do minister.

1 Peter 4:10 (NKJV)
As each one has received a gift, minister it to one another, as good stewards of the manifold grace of God.

Bible Stories
From the Heart

Scripture:_____
_____
_____
_____
_____
_____

Observation:_____
_____
_____
_____
_____
_____

Application:_____
_____
_____
_____
_____
_____

Prayer: _____
_____
_____
_____
_____
_____

Devotion Five

Focus Verses

Psalm 33: 20-22-(NKJV)
20 Our soul waits for the LORD; He is our help and our shield. 21 **For our heart shall rejoice in Him, because we have trusted in His holy name.** *22 Let Your mercy, O LORD, be upon us, just as we hope in You.*

History

Singing spiritual songs and playing music was a common way to worship in Biblical times. There are over 185 songs documented in the Bible. The shortest being only seven Hebrew words long (in Second Chronicles 5:13, 20:21) and the longest being over 1700 words (in Psalm 119).

No matter the length, each song found in the Bible had a specific purpose and goal: each one was sung as a way to REMEMBER God's goodness, to FOCUS on God's truths, to GROW in faith, or to stay ENCOURAGED in times of despair. God knows how easily his children can be distracted from his love and truth. He knows that if this happens, his children can many times be tempted to turn away from him and make bad decisions.

God deeply desires to stay closely connected with us. Songs can help us keep this strong connection. Singing spiritual songs is a good way for God's children to get their focus back on HIM and keep their lives centered on HIS PATH.

Music is a tool provided to us from God.

God created us to respond to music. It is up to us to choose the right kind of UPLIFTING music with which we surround ourselves!

Connection to Us

When we were created, we were designed to feel emotions. It is these emotions which help us bond and connect with our Heavenly Father. It is emotions which keep us human.

We must remember that God created us with the ability to feel emotions. Healthy emotions can be the driving force which propels us toward new goals. Healthy emotions can also be what holds us back from an area that should be avoided.

Emotions are what keep us HUMAN. Emotions keep us pliable and relatable! Emotions themselves are not the problem, the problem comes when we allow temporary emotions to permanently consume us and lead us away from God.

Healthy emotions should guide us CLOSER to God not hinder us or lead us AWAY from our loving Father!

Because emotions have such a pulling force behind them, it is imperative that each one of us look to God to help us focus our emotions. God created His children with the ability to connect with Him. It is this connection that returns us to a feeling of joy even during times of despair. God is LOVE! God is PEACE! God is JOY! The closer we stay to God the more joy and peace we will be able to feel.

It is spiritual songs and singing which can help us RETURN TO GOD'S LOVE, JOY, AND HOPE. Our focus verses today remind us of this. This verse reminds us that our HOPE is in the Lord! No matter what temporary emotion we are feeling, our SOUL is in fact waiting for the Lord! When we find ourselves being consumed with a negative emotion and we begin to feel tempted to pull away from our Heavenly Father, we must keep our HOPE in God! We must WAIT for the Lord to lead us WITH HIS LOVE. We must not react out of emotion!

To help us relax and wait, we must stay connected to God! We must not let our negative emotions consume us and lead us down a dark path. We must do what we can to return to feeling GOD'S LOVE, JOY, AND HOPE.

The right music and singing can help!

By surrounding ourselves with spiritual songs we will be reminded of God's LOVE and NEVERENDING GOODNESS on a daily basis.

It is through these positive reminders that God will be able to gradually guide our emotions back to a sense of HIS peace and JOY! We will remember the pain, but we will not be CONSUMED by the pain. We will be able to transition back to PEACE and once again have a heart which is completely full of joy and totally focused on God!

Focus Words

As you continue in this lesson you will see a reflection activity for you to complete. With this activity, we encourage you to read the entire weekly focus verses again. As you reread the verses, concentrate as deeply as you can on the key words for this activity.

Seek to make personal connections and write them down. Pray to your Heavenly Father to reveal new truths to you. You will be amazed what God will show you through this easy activity. Repeat this activity several times over this coming week.

Reflection Activity

Psalm 33: 20-22-(NKJV)
20 Our soul waits for the LORD; He is our help and our shield. 21 **For our heart shall rejoice in Him, because we have trusted in His holy name.** *22 Let Your mercy, O LORD, be upon us, just as we hope in You.*

Heart- לב *labe:* the *heart*; also used very widely for the feelings, the will and even the intellect.

Rejoice- שמח s âmach: to *brighten* up, to be *gleesome*.

Trusted- בטח *baw-takh':* to *use* for refuge, to *trust*, to be *confident* or *sure*

Name- שם shêm: a mark or memorial of individuality; based on *honor, authority,* or *character*

Connection Activity

Let's read our verse for this week's lesson again and this time we'll exchange some of the focus words for related synonyms:

21 **For our FEELINGS shall BRIGHTEN in Him, because we ARE CONFIDENT in His holy CHARACTER.**

In order to gain confidence in God, a person must do the following things:

1. Fill their mind with information about God, HIS abilities and HIS character. This can be achieved through quality time spent reading and reflecting on scriptures.

2. Constantly focus and remind themselves of what God is capable of. This can be accomplished as a person listens to praise and worship music all throughout their day. As this person focuses on the words in the song, the words can actually help them focus on love and help them regain and maintain their joy.

3. Surround themselves with others who place their confidence in God! This is vital. This can be achieved through joining a Christian small group or Sunday School class near to their home.

We must remember that we CAN take intentional steps throughout our day to ensure that our spirits remain at PEACE. We must also remember that we cannot ever be at peace when we are disconnected from our Heavenly Father! Because of this, we MUST take steps to keep us connected to HIM at ALL TIMES! Listening to spiritual music can help!

Let's focus today on finding favorite spiritual songs to add to our playlists! Let's do our part to remain connected to our Heavenly Father and totally trusting in HIS love for us!

Challenge Activity: If you do not already have a "Spotify" account, I challenge you to create one. They are totally free (unless you choose to enroll in the paid version)

If you do not already have a few favorite spiritual songs, take a few minutes now to "Google" top praise and worship songs. Choose a few to add to your new playlist. Continue to add songs throughout the week that "speak" to a particular area of your heart. Ask God to lead and FILL you with HIS LOVE through the songs that you add.

Rejoice, Rejoice in the Lord
By Deborah Ann Belka

Rejoice, rejoice in the Lord,
be glad and shout out with joy
for He promises to uplift you
and your doubts He'll destroy.

For those who trust in the Lord,
are covered by His mercies
all those who believe in Him
shall conquer their adversities.

Rejoice all who love the Lord,
with delight offer Him your praise
He will shield and protect you
and your fears He will raise.

Stand up against the wicked one,
don't you believe in his lies
all who affirm the work of the Lord
will be blessed with a heart that is wise.

Rejoice in His wonder and glory,
let His splendor embrace you
rejoice and be glad in the Lord
and His love will encircle you too.

For those who rejoice in the Lord,
and give Him their praise each day
are the ones who always trust Him
with His answers when they pray.

Rejoice, rejoice in the Lord,
again I say rejoice . . .
always lift Him up in praise
and let Him hear your voice.

~~~~~~~~~~

https://poetrybydeborahann.wordpress.com

Devotion Five Discussion Questions

1. Why is it important to keep our minds focused on God's goodness?

2. How can music affect our emotions? Do you have a personal experience with a time music affected you- either in a positive or negative way?

3. What do you already know about God's character?

4. What do you hope to discover about God's character?

5. What action steps are you going to take this week to build your confidence in Christ?

Devotion Five Soap Activity

For your weekly SOAP activity, you are encouraged to choose our focus verse from this week or a related verse to reflect deeper upon.

Here are a few choices:

Our focus verse

Psalm 33: 20-22-(NKJV)

20 Our soul waits for the LORD; He is our help and our shield. 21 **For our heart shall rejoice in Him, because we have trusted in His holy name.** *22 Let Your mercy, O LORD, be upon us, just as we hope in You.*

Related verses

Psalm 105: 3-4 (NKJV)

3 Glory in His holy name; Let the hearts of those rejoice who seek the LORD! 4 Seek the LORD and His strength; Seek His face evermore!

Psalm 13:5 (NKJV)

But I have trusted in Your mercy; My heart shall rejoice in Your salvation.

Bible Stories
From the Heart

Scripture: _____
_____
_____
_____
_____
_____

Observation: _____
_____
_____
_____
_____
_____

Application: _____
_____
_____
_____
_____
_____

Prayer: _____
_____
_____
_____
_____
_____

In Him our hearts Rejoice for we trust in His Holy name. Psalm 33:21

Small Scripture Art for Tracing

This is my comfort in my distress- that your promise gives me life.
Psalm 119:50

In Him our hearts Rejoice for we trust in His Holy name.
Psalm 33:21

You also must BE READY because the SON of MAN will COME at an hour when you do not expect HIM.
Luke 12:40

JESUS will always POINT YOU in the Right DIRECTION

the LORD is my STRENGTH & my song HE HAS GIVEN ME VICTORY.
EXODUS 15:2

THANK YOU!

We hope you learned from this study and grew in your knowledge of God's LOVE for you. Thank you so much for supporting our ministry!

Bible Stories from the Heart creates Adult Coloring Bible Studies that help women read and understand the Bible so they will draw near to God and experience His indescribable love in a new, intimate way.

Our studies feature engaging lessons which include; *Bible History, Word Studies, Reflection Activities, Discussion Questions, Art Projects* and *Coloring Pages.*

If you enjoyed this workbook, we hope you will try some of our other studies.

If you haven't already done so, please join our **Bible Stories from the Heart** group on **Facebook**. There, you will join a dynamic, supportive and highly engaged community of thousands of women who participate in our studies and post their artwork to share with other members.

You can find more information on our ministry at: biblestoriesfromtheheart.com.

We would love to hear from you! Please feel to reach us by email with any questions or comments you might have: info@biblestoriesfromtheheart.com.

Thank you!

Made in the USA
Monee, IL
28 May 2022

97151858R10052